This Book
Belongs To

Boo-Boos and Bandages
at School and From Heaven

Eye Chart

by Amy Johnson, BSN, RN-C, School Nurse
A School Nurse for 20 Years

illustrated by
Jennifer Tipton Cappoen

Author: Amy Johnson
Cover Designer and Illustrator: Jennifer Tipton Cappoen
Editor: Lynn Bemer Coble

PCKids is an imprint of **Paws and Claws Publishing, LLC.**
1589 Skeet Club Road, Suite 102-175
High Point, NC 27265
www.PawsandClawsPublishing.com
info@pawsandclawspublishing.com

ISBN #978-1-946198-01-3
Printed in the United States

This book has been written in loving memory of Nurse Greene and Nurse Brown, two beloved school nurses who were not only my co-workers but also my good friends. Both of them were taken too soon from this Earth because of cancer. I feel sure that these two are angels delivering God's bandages.

~Amy Johnson

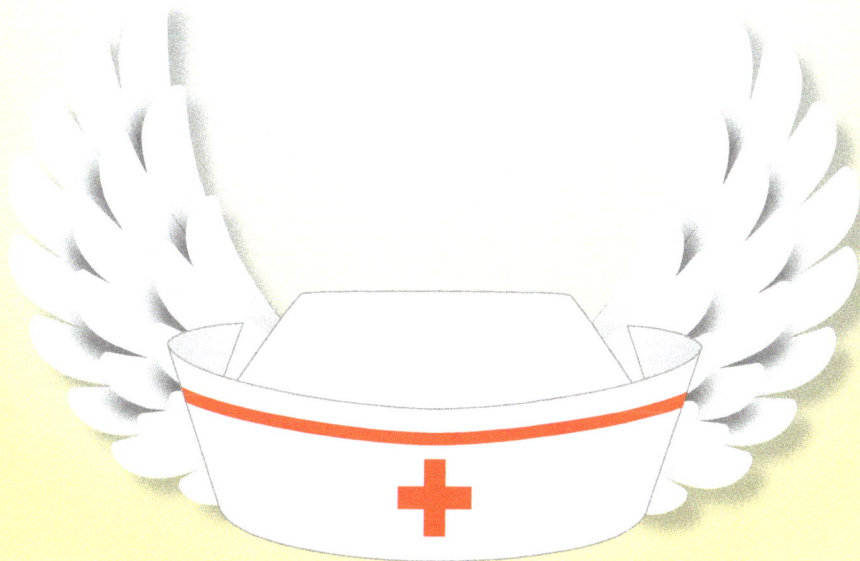

In Memory of
Nurse Deborah "Debbie" Kay Hauser Greene

98.6

She was born December 20, 1952, in Forsyth County to the late Turner Wesley Hauser and Edith Hobson Hauser. Debbie graduated from Forbush High School in 1971 and from the North Carolina Baptist Hospital School of Nursing in 1974.

Nurse Greene was a devoted servant to the public, working for Yadkin County Home Health and Hospice and Yadkin Health Department before finishing her career as a school health nurse for Yadkin County Schools. Debbie impacted many children's lives with her sweet and caring nature.

She was diagnosed in 1996 (when she was 43 or 44) and passed away in 2014, so she fought for 18 years. Nurse Greene continued working for as long as she possibly could, whether it was at kindergarten screening days or at drug screenings. She will be remembered as a brave and resilient fighter with an unparalleled will to live. She received remarkable care from the following: the incredible staff of the Comprehensive Cancer Center at Wake Forest Baptist Medical Center, the staff of the Bone Marrow Transplant Unit, and the dialysis team at Yadkin Dialysis. Hospice started her care in January 2014, and it was the sweet nurse's aide who came in daily who helped the family through those last few months. After a long and courageous battle, Debbie passed away peacefully on April 3, 2014, surrounded by her children.

Debbie will also be remembered as a loving mother of two children and as a devoted grandmother of two grandchildren. She also had four siblings and many nieces and nephews.

In Memory of
Nurse Julia Brown

Julia Brown's legacy of love and passion remain in the hearts of those she touched forever. Through her roles of devoted disciple, loving wife, affectionate momma, sweet granna, faithful teacher, devoted school nurse, and encouraging friend, she spread the love of Christ wherever she went. Spending time with family, teaching children classes at Union Grove Baptist Church, caring for her schoolchildren, tending her garden, and planting colorful flowers brought her great joy.

There are no words to describe the deep ways her sweet spirit and joyful heart are missed. Yet her friends and family rejoice, for we know her joy is fully restored as she now fully lives in the love and presence of her Heavenly Father.

Julia's prayer for each of us can be found in *Ephesians 3:17–21*. May we know the vast love of Christ and look to Him who is able to do exceedingly abundant things above all we ask or think.

Dedication

This book is dedicated to all of the school personnel
who take care of our schoolchildren daily:
school nurses, teachers, teacher assistants, principals,
school secretaries, custodians, bus drivers,
cafeteria workers, media specialists, social workers,
guidance counselors, and more.

And especially to my family and my children,
Tyler and Macy.
Always trust in the Lord.

Kids have accidents that cause boo-boos.
This happens lots of times while they're growing up.

Boo-boos can happen when children play, when
they do schoolwork, or pretty much anytime.

Some kids' boo-boos happen at home.

Others happen at school. At school, accidents can happen in the classroom, in the cafeteria, at recess, in the hallway, or anywhere.

When I was a little girl, I had an accident with a stapler in my classroom. I've treated students who have also hurt themselves with staplers. I've done this a number of times. Many teachers don't allow their students to use the stapler in the classroom for that very reason.

The school nurse isn't always at the school when an accident happens. Many school nurses work in two or more schools. The other adults who work at the school are there to help children who get hurt or are sick when the school nurse is not there.

Teachers, teacher assistants, the school secretary, the principal, and others can also help any student who has an accident, gets sick, or needs medical help. Sometimes these episodes can be scary or embarrassing for the student. All of these adults try to help make the student feel better.

Eye Chart

When blood is involved, first the school nurse or other adult always puts on gloves. That is because we know that you should never touch anyone else's blood.

Then the adult cleans the boo-boo and bandages it. This helps the boo-boo get well. It also keeps out germs.

In some cases, a child's cut or scrape is somewhere that a bandage can't be put on it. It might be on a child's head. Or it could be in his or her hair.

That very thing happened this past school year. I told the young child these things:

1. First we need to clean your boo-boo.
2. You need to keep your hands off the boo-boo because of germs.
3. And you need to wait because God will send an angel with a special bandage to put on the boo-boo. It's called a *scab*. The scab will help the boo-boo heal.

Sometimes the boo-boo is bad enough that it needs stitches or glue done by a doctor. At other times a dentist is needed. For some boo-boos in or around the eyes, the student may need to be seen by an eye doctor.

At other times the boo-boo is minor. Cleaning and a bandage might be all that are needed.

The boo-boo might be a major one on the inside of the child's body. A doctor, a dentist, or an eye doctor may need to find out what is wrong. The child may need X-rays or other treatment.

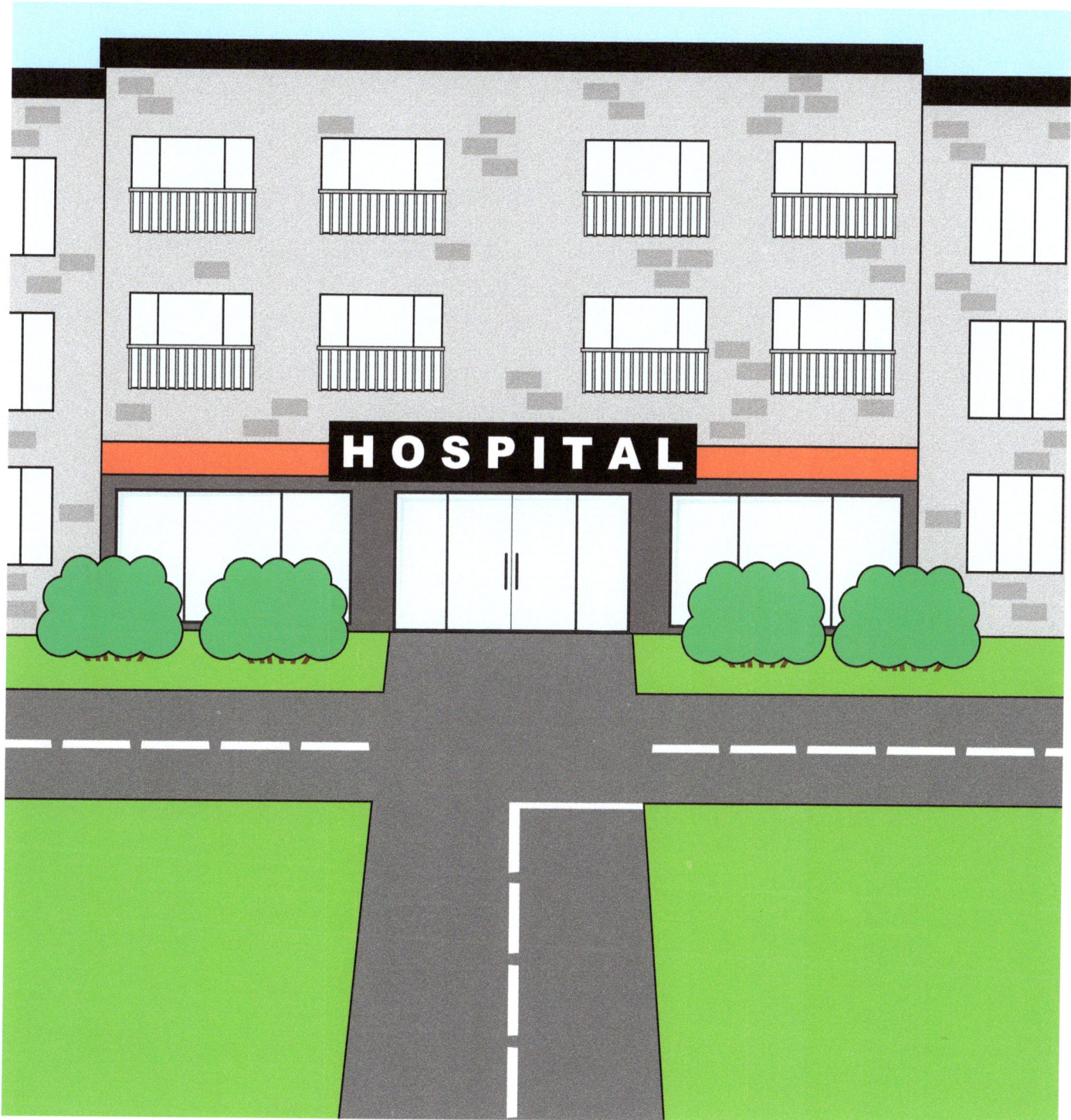

The student may have a broken bone, a sprain, a bad bruise, or some other injury. The child may need a cast, a splint, or a different kind of treatment.

Accidents can happen during sports or at recess. The child may have stumbled, tripped, or run too fast. He or she may have fallen on the slide or monkey bars.

If a student has a possible head injury, this is taken very seriously by the school staff and coaches. It could be a concussion or another type of head injury.

A health-care provider will need to check the child carefully to figure out what is wrong. Doctors and nurses know a lot more now about head injuries in children. They can order the special tests that are needed.

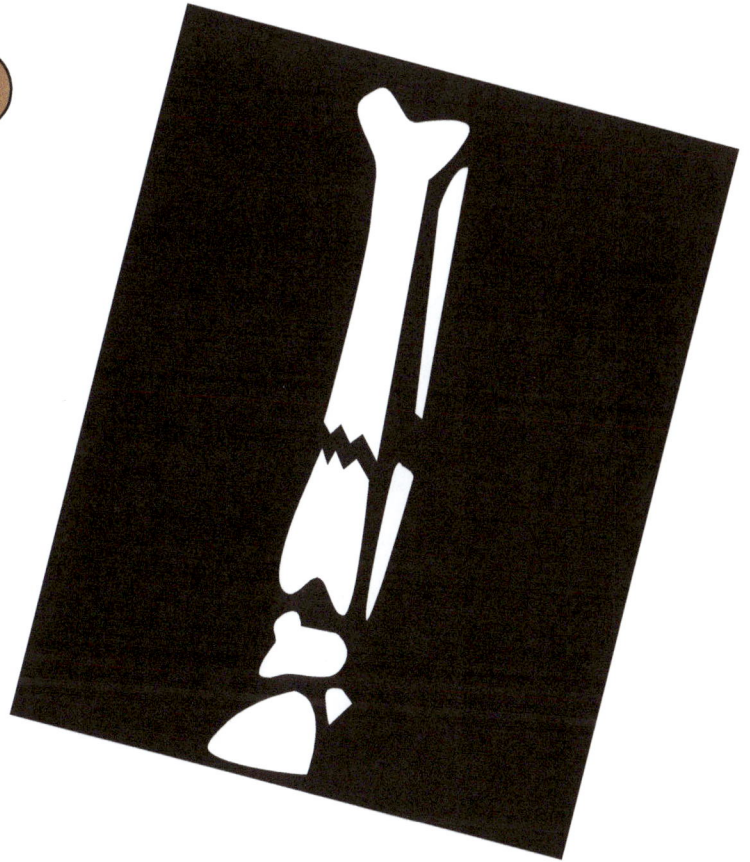

After a child has been taken care of by the school nurse or other adult, that person will complete an accident report. The details of the injury, sickness, or problem are part of that report. It also includes the treatment, outcome, and follow-up.

The school nurse or other adult may contact the child's parent or guardian. This can be done by phone, E-mail, text, or note. The nurse may recommend that the child's parent or guardian seek medical care.

Medical Report

Student: _Jessica Cooper_   Grade: _2_

Parent: _Mr. & Mrs. Dan Cooper_   Date: _May 4_

Teacher: _Mrs. Eakers_   Time: _11:20_

Description of the Incident: _Jessica fell while playing at recess. She has a 2-inch scrape on her left arm. Does not need stitches._

Action Taken: _Cleaned the abrasion and_ _____

_____

_____

_____

Further Recommended Care: _____

_____

Note to Parent: _____

_____

If you have any questions about the above event, please call the school nurse's office.

Most boo-boos heal in time. When the scab falls off, the child can see that the boo-boo is a lot better or is completely gone. This is a small miracle.

Mrs. Eakers, my boo-boo is all healed now.

When you have a boo-boo or feel sick at school, please ask your teacher if you can see your school nurse. A school nurse gives a lot of support and caring, because he or she cares about you.

The school nurse's goal is to help make students feel better. They want the students to be healthy and happy. All adults who work at the school want children to be ready to learn.

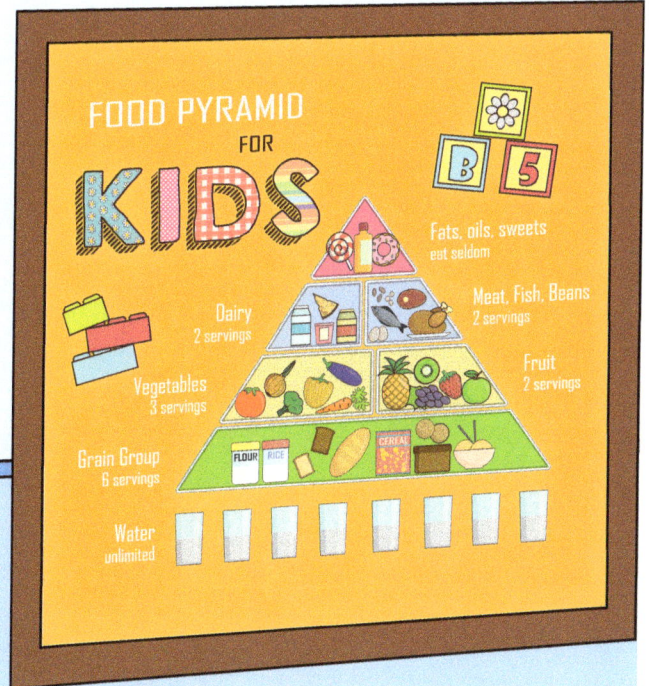

May you all have a blessed and safe day.
I hope you have no accidents and no boo-boos.

What Does A School Nurse Do?

I have been a school nurse in a small, rural system in North Carolina for more than 20 years now. I love being a school nurse because I never know which adult or child is going to walk into the health room and what the issue will be. It may be a small "boo-boo" needing to be cleaned and bandaged or a big issue like a tracheostomy problem. My clients are students and staff of all ages, and they have all made the job of school nurse both enjoyable and challenging. I have collected lots of memories, gotten a lot of hugs, and even cried many tears with my children and co-workers.

Thank you for letting me be your school nurse through both the good and sad times.

School Nurse Duties Include But Are Not Limited To The Following:

- Follow the North Carolina Board of Nursing rules and regulations and the Nursing Practice Act.
- Follow all North Carolina state laws pertaining to School Health and refer to the school health manual often as needed.
- Required to have a bachelor's degree in Nursing. The state of North Carolina also requires that nurses become nationally certified in School Nursing within 3 years of being hired.
- Follow all policies and procedures as set by our local Board of Education.
- (Optional) membership in professional affiliations: SNANC (School Nurse Association of NC) and NASN (National Association of School Nurses).
- Ensure that all students have the state-required immunizations and physicals for public schools.
- Review all health histories each new school year. Let teachers know ASAP about issues.

- Develop IHPs (individual health plans).
- Develop EAPs (emergency action plans).
- Conduct meetings with parents and teachers or other school personnel for special-needs trainings (i.e., tube feedings, diabetic care, catheterizations, etc.).
- Train teachers on how to manage and administer any emergency medications like EpiPen®, Diastat®, etc., when the nurse is not at the school.
- Delegate and train other school personnel to complete tasks and procedures and to administer medications while the school nurse is not at the school. (Most school nurses work in more than one school. This varies from county to county.)
- Document daily encounters of children who visit the nurse for any and all problems.
- Maintain health records.
- Complete wellness screenings (i.e., vision, hearing, etc.).
- Refer any children who do not pass the wellness screenings and make contacts for follow-up.
- Communicate with parents.
- Communicate with other school personnel, especially front-office secretaries and principals.
- Help with any staff and student health issues and injuries during any given school or work day.
- Help with carb counts on nutritional menus for special populations (i.e., diabetics).
- Attend staff-development training sessions.
- Serve on special committees (i.e., SHAC [School Health Advisory Council] and many others).
- Work with any and all communicable-disease issues that might arise during the year. This list of diseases includes flu, pertussis cases, lice, scabies, etc. This list goes on and on.

- Work with mobile dental van when it visits our schools.
- Complete the weekly fluoride mouth-rinse program at the identified schools.
- Complete the required Department of Transportation random drug testing.
- Attend monthly nurse team meetings with our supervisor.
- Complete reports for Department of Public Instruction and Department of Health and Human Services.
- Evaluations of school nurses are done by peer school nurses and principals.
- Teach classes (i.e., human growth and development for 5th-grade girls).
- Teach hands-only CPR. (This is now a graduation requirement in NC public schools.)
- Work with social workers on any special circumstances and sometimes make home visits to speak with parents and/or guardians.
- Educate and refer parents/guardians to outside agencies for resources (i.e., Medicaid/Health Choice, Dental/Primary Care, Food Banks, Clothing, etc.).
- Work with Exceptional Children department.
- Work with guidance counselors on any special circumstances.
- Collaborate with other agencies like Health Departments and the Department of Social Services as needed.
- Maneuver through multiple adolescent issues.
- Our goal is to have kids healthy, happy, and on task ready to learn.

AND especially:
- Lots of listening and hugs for students, parents, and staff who may need them.

~Amy Johnson—School Nurse, RN-C, BSN

About the Author

Amy Johnson has lived in Yadkin County in North Carolina for her entire life, except when she attended college at Western Carolina. She loves to do anything outdoors, including walking, biking, and having time at the lake.

The author earned her Bachelor of Science in Nursing from Western Carolina University. Her first job was in the NICU at Forsyth Medical Center in Winston-Salem. After she left there, Amy worked as a Health Occupations Teacher at Forbush High School in Yadkin County Schools.

For 21 years, Amy worked as the Co-Lead School Nurse for a team of six nurses in the Yadkin County Schools. At the end of her tenure there, she worked at two elementary schools where she provided care to approximately 1,000 students. She loved her babies at her schools and considered them her blessings. Amy was also the Chair of the School Health Advisory Council (SHAC) Committee. She also served on the Epi-Team and Local Emergency Planning Committees for Yadkin County Schools with EMS and the Yadkin County Medical Clinic.

Amy and her husband Zach have been married for 24 years as of August 2016. They're the proud parents of two great kids: Tyler (a junior) and Macy (a freshman), who are both at Appalachian State University now.

Besides her family, the author has a loving mom and dad, a sister and her family, and in-laws and all of their families. Amy has been blessed beyond measure by the good Lord. He has provided her with wonderful friends and family members and a great church.

Losses and trials have been parts of Amy's life journey, but she tries to enjoy every day because life can change in an instant. She's witnessed that firsthand. She misses her retired School Nurses and her two School Nurse friends who succumbed to cancer too young.

Left to right: Tyler, Zach, Amy, Macy, and Andi

www.ingramcontent.com/pod-product-compliance
Lightning Source LLC
Chambersburg PA
CBHW041635040426

42447CB00021B/3497